09
11

10
1

109

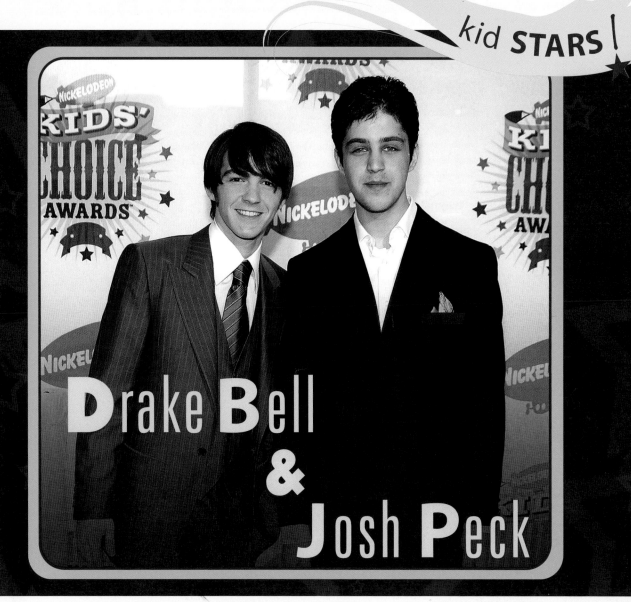

kid STARS!

Drake Bell & Josh Peck

Katie Franks

PowerKiDS press™

New York

Published in 2009 by The Rosen Publishing Group, Inc.
29 East 21st Street, New York, NY 10010

First Edition

Editor: Nicole Pristash
Book Design: Kate Laczynski
Photo Researcher: Jessica Gerweck

Photo Credits: Cover, pp. 1, 4, 7 © Getty Images, Inc.; p.8 © 2007 Zuma Press, Inc./Chris Delmas; p.11 Getty Images, Inc./Kevin Mazur; pp. 12, 15 © Getty Images, Inc.; p. 16 © Associated Press; pp. 19, 20 © Getty Images, Inc.

Library of Congress Cataloging-in-Publication Data

Franks, Katie.
  Drake Bell and Josh Peck / Katie Franks. — 1st ed.
      p. cm. — (Kid stars!)
  Includes index.
  ISBN 978-1-4042-4463-4 (library binding) ISBN 978-1-4042-4534-1 (pbk)
  ISBN 978-1-4042-4552-5 (6-pack)
  1. Bell, Drake, 1986– —Juvenile literature. 2. Peck, Josh, 1986– —Juvenile literature. 3. Actors—United States—Biography—Juvenile literature. I. Title.
  PN2287.B413F73 2009
  792.02'80922—dc22
  [B]
                                                    2007048329

Manufactured in the United States of America

Contents

Drake Bell (left) and Josh Peck (right) first met on the set of the Nickelodeon game show *Double Dare* in 1999.

Meet Drake and Josh

Drake Bell and Josh Peck are the stars of Nickelodeon's *Drake & Josh*. These best friends have been working together since they acted in *The Amanda Show* in 2000. Even when they are not working, these two keep busy. Drake sings and plays guitar. He has made three albums. Josh plays **piano** and **hockey**. He has also been doing stand-up **comedy** since he was eight years old!

Drake and Josh have already accomplished many things. Let's take a look at their life, their work, and what they hope to do next!

Drake Bell

Jared Drake Bell was born on June 27, 1986. He grew up in Newport Beach, which is in Orange County, in southern California. His parents are Joe Bell and Robin Dodson. Drake has a big family, with several brothers and sisters.

Drake started acting at a very young age. He was only five years old when he appeared in a TV **commercial** for Whirlpool. In just a few short years, Drake would begin to play roles, or parts, in movies. One of his earliest movie roles was a small part in *Jerry Maguire* in 1996.

Drake Bell had a lot of big dreams when he was young. He knew he wanted to act in movies and on TV while singing and playing music, too.

Drake is shown here at the first showing of *High Fidelity*.
It took place on March 23, 2000, in Los Angeles, California.

A Budding Talent

In the late 1990s, Drake appeared in small parts on TV shows, such as *Seinfeld* and *The Drew Carey Show*. In 2000, when he was 14, Drake played the child **version** of the main character in the movie *High Fidelity*. With these roles, Drake got the chance to work with many big movie and TV stars.

Drake kept getting parts because of his growing talent as an actor. In 1999, around the same time that he was doing some of this movie and TV work, he joined the cast of *The Amanda Show*. Drake's big break was just around the corner.

The Amanda Show

The Amanda Show played on Nickelodeon from 1999 until 2002. It was a **spin-off** from a show called *All That*. *The Amanda Show* was built around an actress from *All That* named Amanda Bynes. *The Amanda Show* included comedy **sketches**, cartoons, and music. Drake played many different characters on the show.

Another promising young actor became part of the cast in 2000. *The Amanda Show* became Josh Peck's big break just as it had been for Drake Bell. Drake and Josh quickly became good friends while working on the show together.

Amanda Bynes (left), Drake Bell (middle), and Josh Peck (right) worked well together on *The Amanda Show*. They helped bring out each other's funny sides.

As a child, watching actors on TV helped Josh get better at stand-up comedy. He looked up to comedy stars, such as Richard Pryor and Bill Cosby.

Josh Peck

Joshua Michael Peck was born in New York City on November 10, 1986. For the first 14 years of his life, Josh lived in several small apartments in New York City with his mother, Barbara, and his grandmother.

Since childhood, Josh has had **asthma**. This often kept him from being able to run and play outside when he was young. Instead, Josh watched old movies and **sitcoms** on TV. His love of comedy led him to start acting in children's **theater**. He also began doing stand-up comedy when he was just eight years old.

On the Move

Josh did stand-up comedy at places like Caroline's Comedy Club, which is a well-known New York comedy club. His stand-up acts helped raise money for sick children all over the world. His acts also showed people that Josh was very talented and funny.

All this hard work paid off for Josh. In 2000, he appeared in the movie *Snow Day*. Later that year, he was asked to join the cast of *The Amanda Show*. This meant a move from New York to California. Working on *The Amanda Show* let Josh show off his funny side even more.

Josh Peck loves to be onstage and in front of people. Here, he is speaking at the Giffoni Film Festival in Hollywood, California.

Since Drake Bell (left) and Josh Peck (right) are so close, they had a lot of fun making *Drake & Josh*. Here they are seen joking around on the set.

Becoming Drake & Josh

In 2004, two years after *The Amanda Show* ended, Drake Bell and Josh Peck got to work together again, starring in *Drake & Josh*. The idea for the show was based on a sketch from *The Amanda Show*.

Drake and Josh play stepbrothers Drake Parker and Josh Nichols, who are very different from each other. Drake Parker plays guitar and is always talking about girls. Josh Nichols works at a movie theater and likes to stay out of trouble. The show follows their life as they learn to live together and try not to drive each other too mad!

Working Hard

Drake & Josh let its stars shine. The show won a Nickelodeon Kid's Choice **award** in 2006 as the year's favorite show. Drake won the award for favorite TV actor in 2006 and 2007. The show was so **popular** that three TV movies based on the show have been made. They are *Drake & Josh Go Hollywood*, *Drake & Josh: The Really Big Shrimp*, and *Drake & Josh in New York.*

Drake and Josh have kept working in movies, too. Drake appeared in *Yours, Mine and Ours*, while Josh lent his voice to the cartoon *Ice Age 2: The Meltdown.*

Josh Peck (left) and Drake Bell (middle) received the
Nickelodeon Kid's Choice award in 2006 with Miranda Cosgrove (right).
Miranda played Drake's little sister, Megan.

Drake Bell not only sings, he writes all of his own songs, too. Here he is on MTV's *Total Request Live*, in New York City, in 2006.

The show *Drake & Josh* ended in 2007. What's next for its stars? Drake is spending more time on his music. His first two albums came out in 2005 and 2006. More than a million albums were sold. Drake's third album came out in 2008.

In addition to acting, Josh has lost more than 100 pounds (45 kg)! This has helped his asthma and has set a good example of healthy living. Josh is busy making movies. In 2008, he was seen in *The Wackness*, *Drillbit Taylor*, and *American Primitive*. These talented boys will likely be around for years to come!

DRAKE BELL

JOSH PECK

 Drake drives a 1966 Ford Mustang.

 Josh drives a 1987 Mercedes.

 Drake loves to play baseball.

 Josh plays ice hockey in his spare time.

 Drake has a cat named Natasha.

 Josh has a pet fish named Beefy and a dog named Monster.

 Drake's friends sometimes call him The Drakester.

 Josh is 6 feet 1 inch (1.85 m) tall.

Drake is 5 feet 9 ½ inches (1.77 m) tall.

Drake Bell was badly hurt in a car crash in 2005. He had to take time off from making *Drake & Josh* in order to get better.

 Josh likes to make his own hip hop music in his spare time.

Glossary

asthma (AZ-muh) An illness that makes it hard for a person to breathe.

award (uh-WORD) A special honor given to someone.

comedy (KAH-meh-dee) Something funny.

commercial (kuh-MER-shul) A TV message trying to sell something.

hockey (HO-kee) A team game played on ice in which one team uses sticks to try to hit a flat disk, called a puck, into the other team's net.

piano (pee-A-noh) An instrument with small hammers that strike wire strings to make music when its set of keys is pressed.

popular (PAH-pyuh-lur) Liked by lots of people.

sitcoms (SIT-komz) Funny TV shows that have the same group of characters each week.

sketches (SKECH-ez) Short scenes that are generally funny.

spin-off (SPIN-of) A show that is based on the people or setting of another show.

theater (THEE-uh-tur) A building where plays and movies are shown.

version (VER-zhun) Something different from something else.

Index

A
albums, 5, 21
Amanda Show, The,
   5, 9–10, 14, 17
asthma, 13, 21
award, 18

C
comedy, 5, 13–14
commercial, 6

D
Drake & Josh, 5,
   17–18, 21–22

G
guitar, 5, 17

M
movie(s), 6, 9,
   13–14, 18, 21

P
piano, 5

S
sitcoms, 13
sketch(es), 10, 17
spin-off, 10

T
theater, 13

Web Sites

Due to the changing nature of Internet links, PowerKids Press has developed an online list of Web sites related to the subject of this book. This site is updated regularly. Please use this link to access the list:
www.powerkidslinks.com/kids/drajosh/